HOW TO BE BETTER AT BASKETBALL IN 21 DAYS

The Ultimate Guide to Drastically Improving Your Basketball Shooting, Passing & Dribbling Skills

By James Wilson

"When it's played the way is 'spozed to be played, basketball happens in the air; flying, floating, elevated above the floor, levitating the way oppressed peoples of this earth imagine themselves in their dreams."

- John Edgar Wideman

Distinguished American writer and Professor at Brown University on America's love for basketball

DEDICATION

To my parents who raised me in a special basketball environment and taught me about life, courage and that bouncing orange ball.

TABLE OF CONTENTS

INTRODUCTION

Oh, how far thou game have come. It's crazy when you really think about it. Basketball was invented in 1891 by Dr. James Naismith to occupy a group of incorrigibles in his gym class. Then it evolved into leagues like the Eastern Basketball League (1909), the Metropolitan Basketball League (1921), the American Basketball League (1925), and eventually the National Basketball Association (NBA) in 1949. It is not just restricted to the American audience but has also secured a place in World Olympics.

In 121 years, basketball has gone from a single gymnasium, to a mass phenomenon watched and played by millions around the world. Players such as George Mikan, Pistol Pete Marovich, Earl Monroe, Kareem Abdul Jabbar, Magic Johnson, Larry Bird, Michael Jordan, Kobe Bryant, and many more, have helped popularize and evolve the game. They have left permanent marks in the sport.

Now the time has come where you will read *"How to Be Better at Basketball in 21 Days"*, and you will put your own mark, whether it be big or small, on the wonderful game of basketball.

Someone who has arguably put the biggest mark in the game was Phil Jackson. He is the all-time leader of most championships in NBA history and basketball coach of Michael Jordan and Kobe Bryant. He once said, *"It's not how hard you play and train that matter it's how smart."*

Phil was absolutely right. Too often players spend countless hours on the basketball court and in the weight room working as hard as they possibly can, yet they see little to no improvement. They simply don't have the proper guidance, or are misinformed on how to fully utilize their true potential.

This book will teach you **how to become the best basketball player that you can possibly become in** a short period of time i.e. **21 days**. You will learn fundamentals, drills, and exercises that are used by top NCAA and NBA basketball players.

Whether you play for fun, or play at the High School, College, or Professional level, this program will benefit you. If you read everything carefully, work as hard as you possibly can every day, and stick to the program without missing any workouts, I promise you that in 21 days, you will have the skill set, finesse and confidence to give a very challenging time to your opponents.

We won't have much time but we have much to accomplish, so we have divided the training into three modules that are all related to each other and will help you become a much better basketball player. Before we start our training we want to make sure you have the right approach in the game. An introductory chapter precedes your first module and is all about preparation for a successful season. We want to lay emphasis on the importance of *mental preparation*. Our mind controls our body, thus adjusting our mindset and playing with a trouble free mind are vitally important for a successful game.

The first module is *"Understanding The Game"*. This chapter teaches fundamentals, techniques, and theories on how to become a better shooter, dribbler and passer. You will also learn the tools for improving your athleticism and conditioning, and how to prevent injuries and recover fully. You will discover the precise techniques professionals use.

- How to increase your basketball shooting accuracy?

- What are the most effective ways to improve your dribbling skills?

- How to improve your passing skills in basketball?

Those are just few of the questions you will find the answers to in this chapter.

While the first module was raw techniques and fundamentals, the second module is dedicated for ***drills and exercises*** that are based off everything taught in the first chapter. They will specifically help you become a better dribbler, shooter, passer, and increase your athleticism.

The third module is particularly designed for **The 21 Day Program**. This module provides in-depth instructions for every day and uses all of the drills and exercises that we explained in the module before. In order to participate in the program, you will need a pair of basketball shoes, a basketball, a basketball court, and a stopwatch.

Throughout the book we have included interesting pictures, quotes and some video links for your reference. Moves that require illustration have been supported with pictures so you will have a better understanding of the theory.

You will be tested to your limits but on the last day you will notice a marked change in your playing style, your shooting would be more on the spot and your navigation around the court will have dramatically improved.

The world of basketball is quite fascinating and this book can make the difference between average players and seasoned professionals in a matter of 21 days!

Let us begin.

PREPARING FOR A SUCCESSFUL SEASON

Summer is almost over and you do not have much time left to prepare for the coming season, so as a varsity or college player you need to start getting into form!

What is form? We all know that it has something to do with staying fit, healthy and in good physical shape to take on the opponent mercilessly on the court but do you know that it has a lot to do with your attitude? Our mind controls our body, thus adjusting our mindset and playing with a trouble free mind are a very important part of the game as you will soon find out.

This chapter deals with our *mental conditioning* at the start of a season or even before an everyday friendly game.

Knowing Your Basketball Philosophy

"I have no individual goals. We play for one reason and that's to win the title. Practice is more important than the games, and I will practice when I'm hurt, when 95 percent of the players in this league would sit out. I expect all of you to do the same thing. You will follow my lead."

– Michael Jordan

Just like your college or high school motto every basketball team in the world is led by a philosophy that reflects the core ideas that lay at the heart of its foundation. This philosophy guides your decision making and gives you the 'way forward' during your time with the team.

Remember, philosophy is not about winning. Winning is a byproduct of your team's conduct and values, an inevitable outcome of you holding true to your motto. For Chicago Bulls under the leadership of Michael Jordan it was '***practice makes perfect***'.

Many times the philosophy of a team transcends the usual measures of success, such as a nice clean game or a comfortable lead on the scoreboard. Coaches of these basketball teams lay great emphasis on a team game, effective communication among players and respect. They say that a **successful basketball team is one where**:

- The agendas and intentions of all team members is the same.

- Defeat is accepted with dignity and lessons are learned from mistakes.

- Discipline is observed by everyone.

- Dedication and giving in an extra effort is observed.

Thus the philosophy of these teams is that their team members transform into better human beings rather than the basketball monsters from the movie '*Space Jam!*' When that happens, everyone becomes a winner irrespective of the score.

These were just a few examples of a team's philosophy. A simple way to determine what your team's philosophy is to ask yourself: *what is the most important message I take home with me after every season?*

Mental Attitude

Determining your team's philosophy gives you and your team a head start in preparing for game day. You are more focused now but more importantly you are coming with the right frame of mind to start practicing for the new season.

Although the team's vision might not be very easy to grasp there is one aspect of practice that even the slowest of people can excel at without much thinking and that is **conditioning**. This is because your conditioning is something you have complete conscious control over, it does not depend much on funding, team morale, management issues, troubles at home. While these things do play a role in your life the fact remains that the more your practice self discipline the better you get. This is entirely up to you.

The world is a very competitive place and no one can ignore this reality. It is no secret that everybody likes a winner. But what happens often during competitive sports is that the focus of the game spirit shifts from merits of the game to an all-out war. Fist fights, brawls among audience, spot fixing and gambling are some of the consequences when sports turn into an industry.

> *"If you make every game a life-and-death thing, you're going to have problems. You'll be dead a lot"*
>
> *— Hall of Fame Coach Dean Smith*

Winning is important, but only the kind where every player feels that he or she is putting in the best effort. There is no shame in losing nor does a victory feel more deserved after a game where every player has put in a 110%. Yes we are talking about gaming ethics. When players know that they have worked hard all season it is easier to motivate them with pep talks, they are more receptive to advice and the team plays as a coherent whole.

Practice, hard work, honesty and team spirit are the ingredients of a correct attitude. Most of you will not make it to the NBA but you will know that you gave in your best. This lesson will stick with you in your professional lives, when you become an important part of a corporation or when you start an innovative business. This attitude will change your life for the better.

Visualizing Your Game

Now maintaining focus, holding true to your conditioning and practice will go a long way to improve your game but there is an aspect of the game that coaches often do not take into account and something that can give a significant boost to your skills; that something is known as **visualization**.

Michael Jordan once said, *"I visualized where I wanted to be, what kind of player I wanted to become. I guess I approached it with the end in mind. I knew exactly what type of player I wanted to become."*

Young Michael Jordan

Research has shown that *people who meditate and think about every aspect of the game in their heads are better prepared for the game environment* when the moment of truth arrives. This only makes sense because, your mind controls your body, practice will condition your muscles to repeat a proper movement but the visualization will give your muscles the proper coordinates, that subtle extra push of your feet, the gentle nudge of your wrist that finally gets the ball through that net!

So what you need to do is sit in your room, with dim lights before bed time preferably, because that's when you are most relaxed. Now think about yourself standing at the free throw line, about to shoot the ball, imagine the feel of the ball in your hands, imagine the noisy spectators and imagine your team mates yelling at you. Visualize seeing the ball as it leaves your hand and glides towards the net in a perfect backspin. Finally, visualize your hands in a perfect follow up. Practice this scenario in your head every day for 10 minutes. Watch game plays of your team as well as professional NBA players battling on the court so you have images stored in your head for later use.

Visualizing your goals is an important motivational skill and has much to do with the **law of attraction**. It is a very important theory to be successful in whatever endeavor you undertake in life, be it business, management, sports, counseling etc.

According to this theory a person is a magnet that draws only what he/she desires the most. 'Like desires like', in short. The idea is to expunge all negatives aspects of your game from your mind and only focus on the positive aspects of your game.

Visualize, enhance and focus on your strengths and eventually they will get stronger and easily overpower all your weaknesses.

Now that you have the perfect mindset, let's figure out how to improve your game!

UNDERSTANDING
THE GAME

Before we start our first round of training let's talk about some of the mistakes that players frequently make. These four mistakes are the most common rookie mistakes that varsity players make and that sometimes even professionals overlook.

Common Mistakes Basketball Players Make

1. **Playing competitive tournaments all year round.**

   We can understand that many of you love playing a game and drive satisfaction out of it but competitive games off season, with AAU, street tournaments etc. will lower your learning curve. You should take time out for exercise, tactics and conditioning too!

2. **Over looking core strength.**

   Your core strength comes from the hips, abdominals, waist and the back. Every movement in the body involves these muscles to some extent. Since basketball is a hard hitting sport and requires stability your hips and back should be lose, your lower back must be very strong. Weight training to improve the core shouldn't be ignored.

3. Improving vertical by over doing Plyometrics.

Many players work on the vertical movements by concentrating very hard on Plyometrics. These exercises are very taxing for the knee and continuous training without adequate strength can cause serious injuries.

4. Long distance training is ideal for conditioning.

Even though hard facts are present against long distance and marathon training for basketball conditioning coaches and parents still focus on these methods. Let us say once and for all that aerobic activities such as this will only make you lose a ton of weight and nothing more.

Ball Handling and Dribbling

Ball handling lies at the core of your basketball game. Good ball handling means you have better control of the ball, which in turn means that you have a strong foundation to shoot, pass or dribble.

First off, get yourself as familiar with the ball as possible. This means you have the basketball in your hands around your house, in the backyard, out in the streets or the school gym.

Before you begin dribbling, you must understand the **triple threat position**. It is the first thing that any basketball player should learn. Anytime someone passes you the ball it should become your instinct to quickly put the ball into the triple threat position.

The triple threat position is when you are in a crouched, athletic, attack stance, you have a firm grip on the ball near your right or left hip (not in front of you or above your head), and your eyes are facing forward and you are able to see everything that is happening on the basketball court. Once you are in this position, you instantly become a threat because you are able to accurately do 1 of 3 things; you can pass, shoot or dribble – hence the name, the triple threat position.

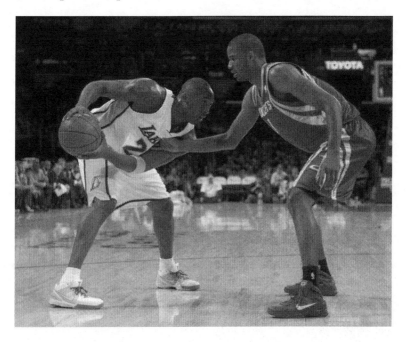

The *triple threat position* is important because it **allows you to shoot, dribble, or pass, as quick as you possibly can** - before the defense can get set and be ready to guard you. Basketball is played at a quick pace (depending on where you play, there may be a shot clock), so it is important to do everything as efficiently as possible and not waste valuable time.

If you were to just stand however you wanted to, not be in an attack ready position, and wave the ball around carelessly, then it would be easy for players to steal the ball from you. You will also slow the pace of the game down by having to re-adjust yourself when you want to shoot, pass, or dribble.

Remember, whenever someone passes you the ball, it should become a habitual instinct (without thinking), to put the ball into your triple threat position!

Now that you understand the triple threat position, it is important to grasp these **quick tips about dribbling**.

o   Whenever you dribble the basketball you want to be *touching the ball with your fingertips* and NEVER with the palm of your hand. This gives you the best possible control of the ball.

o   The correct position to dribble is knees bent and shoulder width apart, keeping your back straight. Your *head should always be up* and eyes out in front so you can see everything that is happening on the court. NEVER stare downwards at the ball.

o   Dribbling is always done both on your *right side or your left* but NEVER in front of you.

o   You want to *keep your hand on the ball as long as possible* (fully extend your arm on every dribble and get your hand as low to the ground as possible). If someone tries to steal the ball from you and your hand is on the ball you can change the direction of the ball to avoid their hands. However, as soon as you let go of the ball it is out of your control.

o   *Protect the ball with your opposite hand.* If someone tries to reach in and steal the ball, you can block their hand away with your opposite hand.

o   *Practice with both hands!* You will need to use both hands in a real basketball game so get comfortable using both of your hands when you practice.

Before you learn how to do crossovers, you must master ***the basic 3 dribbles***. These are the foundations to any good dribbler. All top NBA players have these three dribbles mastered.

The Control Dribble

The control dribble is the standard dribble. This dribble is used at slow and mid-speed. You must get a wider and lower base, crouching lower to the ground while dribbling the basketball lower to the ground. Use your body, legs and opposite arm to shield the basketball and protect it from being stolen. Anytime you drive by someone, or do a crossover, you should be using your control dribble.

Speed Dribble

The speed dribble is used as you are running at top speed, dribbling down the court. For this dribble, you are basically throwing the ball in front of you and running and catching up to it. You fully extend your arm forward and then flick your wrist down.

Power Protection Dribble

This dribble is used anytime someone gets extremely close to you. You want turn your body to the sideways as you dribble and get low to the ground. This creates space between you and your opponent so it is harder for them to steal the ball. The lower the dribble the harder is for the defender to steal it and easier for you to control it.

NOTE: It is important to master all of these three dribbles and be able to transition between them comfortably. For example, you should be able to run at top speed using your speed dribble, then as you reach midcourt transition into your control dribble, then transition into your power protection dribble if your defender gets too close to you.

SITUATION: Someone passes you the ball.
You catch it and immediately put it into your triple threat.
Now, you want to get by your defender. How do you do it?

Answer: When you are in your triple threat position,
there are two basic ways to get around someone without
simply dribbling and then going into a crossover. You should
attempt to use these moves before doing any crossovers.

The first way is ***the basic rip through drive***. You rip the ball in front of you and off to the side a bit, as you drive by your opponent. You want to make sure you rip the ball low to the ground so it will be difficult for your defender to steal. You want to drive in as straight as line possible and try to blow by your defender.

The second way is ***the jab fake, rip through drive***. This is the same as the rip through drive, except you fake going in one direction, then you go the other way. They key to this is really making it look as if you are going to go in one direction, then go the other way. You can make it look as if you are going in the direction by jabbing quickly with your foot, and entire body, and by faking with the ball. You want to make sure you dribble the ball on the ground before you lift your pivot foot off the ground, otherwise it will be a travel.

Crossovers

Now that you understand how to get the ball into the triple threat position and drive off the dribble. It is important to know **how to do a crossover**. What is a crossover? *A crossover is when you are dribbling the basketball in one hand and you fake like you are going to go in one direction, then you quickly switch the ball to the other hand and go in the opposite direction.* Read these ***crossover tips*** before you get started!

- In order to have a good crossover, you have to really sell the fake. Your opponent has to really believe that you are going to go in the direction that you want him to think you are going in. How do you do this? The simplest way to do this is to practice and literally make your crossovers look identical to what you would do if you were actually going in that direction. This may be hard at first, but with enough practice it will become effortless.

- Move the ball as quick as you can. This is essential to a good crossover. You want to do every crossover extremely quick so your defender will have a hard time reacting and cutting you off. No matter how quick your running and explosive speed is, if you can't do a quick enough crossover to keep up, then you will have problems.

- Keep your head up so you can see what is happening around you on the basketball court and use your opposite hand to protect the ball from your defender reaching in.

- Go in a straight line. The quickest way from point A to point B is in a straight line. When you are trying to go around your defenders attack them at straight on angles. Don't run in a curve and try to get around them.

- Always be under control!

These are **the basic four and a half fundamental crossovers** that are used in basketball. Each crossover has a specific time that it should be used. Any other double or triple crossovers are based off using these four and a half crossovers. *Master these four and a half crossovers and you will become a master of dribbling.*

1. *The basic left to right, or right to left crossover.* This is simply dribbling with one hand and then switching to the other. It's simple, but extremely effective. It should be used whenever you have enough space between you and your defender so that they cannot steal the ball.

2. ***The between the legs crossover.*** This crossover should be used when you are closer to your defender and the ball would get stolen if you were to use a regular left to right/right to left crossover.

3. ***The behind the back crossover.*** This crossover should be used when your defender is extremely close to you. You do not have enough space to do a regular crossover or between the legs crossover.

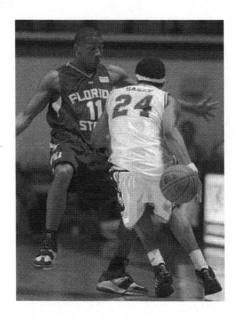

4. *The spin crossover.* This should be used when the defender is extremely close to you and they are already leaning a bit in one direction. Whatever way they are leaning, you simply do a spin and rotate around them in the opposite direction.

5. *The half crossover,* the in and out. This is a good crossover to use when you want to fake using a screen and go in the opposite direction. It is also a great setup for a double crossover, but can be used at any time to get around someone (if there is enough space).

Double and triple crossovers are used if your defender cuts you off after you have done you first crossover. If this happens, you simply do another crossover (double crossover), and if you get cut off one more time, you do another crossover (triple crossover). Double and triple crossovers consist of any combinations of the four and a half fundamental crossovers.

Shooting

Offense wins matches and at the core of every offense lie good shooters. If you analyze some of the greatest shooters of all time, from Reggie Miller, to Ray Allen, to Michael Jordan, you will notice that all of them shoot the basketball with different technique, yet, they are all great shooters. Therefore, it is not about what technique you use to shoot the basketball, but what qualities your technique allows you to have. If your basketball shooting technique allows you to have these three qualities, you will instantly be a great shooter.

1. *Fast Release*. If you can't release the ball fast enough players will block your shot. Therefore, you need to be able to release the ball as quick as you can to avoid players from contesting or blocking your shot.

2. *Accuracy*. This is plain and simple, you need to be able to accurately shoot the ball and get it in. Whether it is to bank the shot off the backboard, or simply shoot the ball in the net, you need accuracy.

3. *Consistency*. You need to be able to consistently get the ball in the net. This is achieved by shooting with the same technique every time.

If your technique allows you to have these three qualities, it doesn't matter if your shot looks ugly or pretty, *you will be a great shooter.* Think about it, if you can shoot the ball so quick that no one can block you, and you consistently get the ball in every time, how are you not a great shooter?

That being said, there is a general technique that nearly every single high school, NCAA, and NBA player uses, that allows them to shoot the ball accurately, consistently, and fast.

You are about to learn the **basketball shooting technique** that has been passed down from generation to generation and **used by many NBA players**. However, take into consideration, if you are trying to emulate a professional, that even if you are using identical technique, everyone's shot will look different because of their height, bodyweight, limb lengths, and proportions. That being said, just because your shot may not look exactly like Michael Jordan's or Ray Allen's, it doesn't mean that you aren't a great shooter!

When you are learning your basketball shooting technique, always remember what you want your technique to produce – a fast release, accuracy, and consistency.

Step 1: Shooting stance.

Get into your triple threat position, face your feet and body to the net, make sure your torso is completely upright (not leaning in any direction), and stare at the rim. It doesn't matter if you stare at the front, back, or entire rim. Every player is different. Choose whatever you feel comfortable doing and stick to it!

Your feet should be about shoulder width apart, however, some people may be wider or narrower depending on personal preference. The important thing is to be in a comfortable position where you are balanced and able to comfortably jump and shoot. Many right handed NBA players prefer to have their right foot slightly ahead of their left foot, and left handed players prefer to have their left foot slightly ahead of their right. The stronger leg will take charge of your jump.

You want your torso in a completely upright position. Another words, you don't want to be leaning too far forwards, backwards, or to the side. This is one quality that Ray Allen has that separates him from other players. His torso stays completely upright throughout his entire shot.

It doesn't matter what type of shot you are shooting (3 point, free throw, shooting off screen, step back, pull up), before you leave the ground, you should be in your triple threat position, your body and feet should face the net and your eyes focused on the rim, and your torso should be upright and balanced.

Step 2: Holding the ball.

NOTE: *You are currently in your triple threat position with your feet and body facing the net, your eyes are focused on the rim, and your torso is upright and balanced.*

First, spread your fingertips so they cover a comfortable amount of the ball. REMEMBER: *The ball should be* **on your fingertips** *and not touching your palm.* This allows for optimum control.

Second, you should have your shooting hand placed in the middle of the ball (right hand for right handed people, left hand for left handed people), and your guide hand resting on the side of the ball. REMEMBER: *You do not actually shoot the ball with your guide hand.* It is only used to hold onto the ball and help aim or "guide" the shot.

Third, your *fingertips should be lined up perpendicular to the seams of the basketball.* This allows the ball to get a perfect backspin upon release, which will help increase its trajectory and also increase its chances of going in if it bounces off the rim. However, even the best NBA players don't always line their fingers up perpendicular to the seams. If the shot clock is running down, or someone is close to them and they do not have enough time, they will just shoot the ball however it is resting in their hands. Don't ever line your fingers up perpendicular to the seams if it means sacrificing a fast release and puts you in jeopardy of getting blocked.

RIGHT   WRONG

Step 3: The two 90 degree hooks.

NOTE: *You are currently in your triple threat position with your feet and body facing the net, your eyes are focused on the rim, your torso is upright and balanced, your shooting hand is spread out on the middle of the ball (lined up perpendicular to the seams if you have enough time), and your guide hand is spread out on the side of the ball.*

Next, you need to create two 90 degree hooks.

First, you need to bend your wrist backwards until it goes to roughly 90 degrees; *this is the first 90 degree hook.*

Second, you want to bend your forearm backwards, until the point where your forearm and bicep meet creates roughly a 90 degree angle; *this is the second 90 degree hook.*

So at this point, you should have two 90 degree hooks, one at your wrist, and one in your arm. You should create these hooks before you even begin to rise up and shoot. This will set you up for a fast release.

Step 4: Rising up.

NOTE: You are still in your triple threat position with your feet and body facing the net, your eyes are focused on the rim, your torso is upright and balanced, your shooting hand is spread out on the middle of the ball (lined up perpendicular to the seams if you have enough time), your guide hand is spread out on the side of the ball, and you have created two 90 degree hooks with your hand and arm.

You will now raise the ball up towards your head as you simultaneously begin to jump.

You want your torso to maintain its upright position. You will bring the ball up in a completely straight line from your feet all the way up to your head. Your shooting elbow should be under the ball and in alignment with your foot, knee, and hip.

You will maintain the two 90 degree hooks the entire time as you are bringing the ball towards your head and beginning your jump. Just before your feet leave the ground and the ball is near the top of your head, you will reach your "*set point*". This is the point that you stop at before you extend your arm and flick your wrist to shoot. You will actually stay in your set point for a fraction of a second until you reach the top of your jump and release your shot. Every player has a different set point. Someone like Kevin Garnett's set point is actually behind his head. However, the majority of NBA player's set points are slightly above their head and in front of their face. Play around and find a comfortable set point and stick to it!

Step 5: Leaving the ground and releasing the shot.

NOTE: You are now in your set point and about to leave the ground and rise into the air.

Your feet and body will now leave the ground and you will rise into the air. You keep the ball and your entire body in the exact same position that it was in before you left the ground, until you are near the top of your jump. You do not want to be leaning in any direction.

Once you are near the top of your jump you will extend your arm upwards into the air and flick your wrist downwards as you keep your fingertips spread, and the ball leaves your hands towards the net. Your fingers should end up like a fish hook, pointing towards the ground. You want to time your shot so that the ball leaves your hands when you are at the top of your jump (highest point in the air).

The TV show *"Sports Science"* calculated that the optimum angle of release that your arm should be at when you shoot is 46 to 50 degrees. After the ball leaves your hands, many top coaches teach their players to "hold their release". This means that you maintain the same position that you had when the ball left your hands. This will allow you to get a good follow through and enables you to analyze your shot. For example, you can look at your arm/wrist/fingers and see if the angle of your arm was too high/low/far to the right/far to the left, and to see if your wrist was bent down enough and your fingers were spread out enough.

Step 6: Analyzing the shot.

The ball has left your hands and it will have done one of two things; go in, or miss. No matter what happens, every time after you shoot, you want to analyze what happened. Think about what you did wrong and what you did right. Learn from any mistakes you made and make the proper adjustments for the next shot you take.

TIP: Get a video camera and record yourself shooting. By doing this, you will pick up on many details that you wouldn't have noticed from shooting without a camera. Sometimes you think your body is doing one thing, but it is actually doing something completely different. A camera can end up saving you a lot of time when learning how to shoot properly. Many top NCAA and NBA players have analyzed videos of their shots at some point or another in their careers.

Taking the Free Throw Shot

Now a free shot may look like it is the easiest shot of the game because there is no defense. But the absence of defense is the very reason why the shot is so difficult. When you are standing on the free shot line all eyes are on you, you have to come up to the expectations of your teammates and the audience and you are feeling the true power of the game, which is very different from practice. But here is what *Michael Jordan* says is the **right way for free shooting**:

1- Make sure you have your balance. It does not mean that both of your feet must be parallel. Some players keep their right feet or the left feet slightly ahead to maintain proper balance.

2- As you get into balance you must clear your mind of the game and think about your practice sessions. That way you will be relaxed and comfortable. This is very important.

3- Once you have the balance you have three choices for focal points, i.e. your target: the rim, inside the rim or back of the rim.

4- When you raise your hand the ball must be on your fingertips, while your forearm should be vertical. The ball should not be on your palms, since that will lessen your control over the ball.

5- When taking the shot try to force your first three fingers from the thumb to work more than the last two. This will create backspin and increase the possibility of the ball going in the basket if it hits the rim.

6- While shooting the force must come from your feet, transfer through the rest of your body and release through your fingers as you take the shot.

7- Lastly, make free shooting into a ritual and only use the same set of movements every time you take a shot. For Michael Jordan it was spinning the ball once, dribbling it three times and spinning it again right before taking the shot.

Mastering Long Range Shooting

The coveted 3 point shooting is considered the epitome of basketball shootings. Taking of the shot on the game bell and making a perfect 'swish' with the ball is a finale akin to a boxing knockout win. Let's look at some *advanced basketball shooting tips*:

Eyes on the Rim!

Shouldn't the title say eye on the ball? Well, no. The aim of dribbling and ball handling exercise is to get as much 'eye time' away from the ball as possible. We want you to focus on anything but the ball and the more your practice the less frequent you will need to look at the ball.

Instead, as a shooter we want you to keep your attention on the rim. Always know exactly where the rim is because then your brain subconsciously keeps the angle and distance calculation. This increases your focus and increases the chance of making the basket when you actually shoot.

Proper Finish

After you have taken the shot it is very important to have the correct follow through. Your wrist should be relaxed and not tense. The entire motion from the shooting to follow up should be one fluid movement.

Before the start of each game or practice, try shooting 50 shots from the free throw line to get the feel of a shot.

Do Not Try to Shoot Like Kobe Bryant

Kobe Bryant is not an ordinary basketball player; an all-star player who lives and breathes basketball with thousands of hours of practice under his belt. Do not mimic him and stick with the basics. Shoot as you are going up and release the ball at the top of your jump.

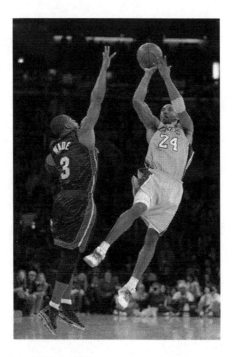

Avoid Thinking about Your Shot

Never think about shot mechanics during the game. A game is not the time to analyze your skill or technique. Just like a final exam you should be more concerned about winning the game and scoring rather than tip and technique. That is done during practice.

If you do want to think, think that it doesn't matter if you make the basket. If it does make the basket congratulate yourself and move on. If it does not, tell yourself that it was a nice try and you will make it next time.

Tips like these are important for your game psyche and natural form.

Practicing of shooting drills

Instead of standing waiting to shoot hoops try to restrict shooting the ball to only after an exhaustive drill. This will test how well you perform in the middle of the game. In fact this is the only way shooting drills should be practiced during a practice.

Passing

Basketball is a team game. All of the five players should work as cogs in a wheel, each relying on one another for support, while making sure they do their part most efficiently.

Your team strength may not lie in shooting killer hoops or blocking impossible ones from the opposite side but if you have good coordination and trust among each other your ball possession is going to increase many folds and hence the chances of scoring.

And yet we see passing as a very under taught aspect of the sport. Passing has been reduced to a matter of necessity only when a player does not see an opening for a shot. This attitude will not do and you need to work hard to improve coordination, skill, trust and ball handling to make your team a disciplined family.

Just like shooting, it is not necessarily about how good your technique is, but what qualities your passing technique allows you to have. You want your passes to be **accurate, fast, and consistent**. You want to be able to pass the ball accurately to your teammate's hands, you want to be able to pass the ball fast enough to them so that no one will steal the ball, and you want to be able to do this consistently - every single time.

Major Types of Passes

The **chest pass** is made from the chest and is the most common pass in basketball. You want to place your thumbs near to back of the ball and then extend your arms forward and snap your thumbs down (towards the ground) and face your palms outwards. The ball should be thrown at the receiver's chest.

The **bounce pass** uses the exact same technique as the chest pass, however, you bounce the ball against the floor first, to sneak the ball between defenders arms. You want to bounce the ball 2/3 of the way between yourself and your teammate. If you bounce the ball closer than this, the ball will slow down and be floating in the air for a long time, making it easy for the defender to steal. A bounce pass should reach the player in a single bounce at about waist height.

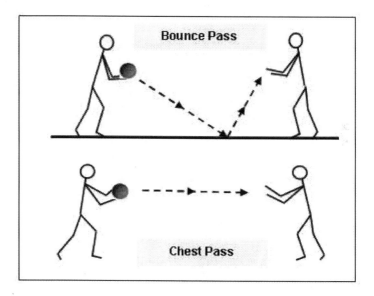

The **overhead pass** uses the exact same technique as the chest pass, however, you do it from over the top of your head. Your fingers still end up pointing towards the ground and your palms facing outwards. This pass is used when you need to pass to defenders far away from you, or skip the pass across the three point line, over defenders heads, to your teammates.

Aim for the receivers chin and don't take the ball behind your head.

The **dribble pass** is used to quickly transfer the ball with one hand to a nearby teammate while dribbling. This move takes practice to master. Steve Nash is often seen practicing this move.

The **baseball pass** is made when the ball has to travel an extremely long distance. You throw the ball just like a baseball. This is an advance pass and rigorous practice must be made first before using it.

Defense

All coaches have different theories on how to play defense. Therefore, it becomes difficult and almost pointless for us to give you specific assignments on how to guard someone. We could tell you one thing, and your coach tells you another.

Some coaches will tell you to force the player you are guarding to the outside of the court; other coaches will say to the middle of the court. Some coaches will want to you to defend a player close; other coaches will want you to sag off the player. Some coaches will want you to play your man full court on defense; other coaches will want you to pick them up at half court. Some coaches will play man defense; other coaches will play zone. Some coaches will want you to help out your teammates if they get beat on defense; other coaches will tell you never to leave the player you are guarding.

In general, each coach has their own theory, and there are endless different assignments that a coach can give a player. Therefore, we will explain the basic principles and techniques that will allow you to *play optimal defense* and *properly execute whatever assignment your coach gives you*!

Defensive Stance

The first thing to learn is the proper defensive stance. While maintaining a defensive stance, balance is key. Anyone can stand with arms spread out but few have the right balance to provide formidable resistance. Here are the key features of a defensive basketball position:

- Your feet must be spread out wider than shoulder length since that will provide your body a firm base.

- Your weight must be borne by the balls of your feet but the heels must be in contact with the ground at all times.

- Your back should be as straight as possible so you have the strength of the back in your stance as well.

- Knees should be bent slightly inwards and in a half squat position for greater push power.

- Your torso leaning forward slightly and your arms spread wide apart.

The Defensive Slide

Whenever you move left to right **your feet should never crossover each other**! Instead you point your lead foot in the direction you are going in (if you are moving left, then your left foot is your lead foot and vice versa), and then you lift your lead off the ground and push yourself (slide) by using force from your other leg.

The Defensive Change of Direction

Whenever your defender changes directions, you must also. You do this by planting your outside foot, and then pivoting and changing directions. You want to make the plant and pivot as quick as possible.

Boxing Out

Whenever someone shoots the ball, you do NOT want to go and chase after it. Instead, you want to find the player you are defending, place your forearm on them so they can't get around you, and then pivot around and jam your butt into their leg. This will stop them from getting the ball. This is called boxing out and all coaches expect their players to do this instead of just chasing the ball. If everyone on the team boxes out their defenders then it increases their chances of getting the rebound.

Middle of the Court Rule

Never let the opponent play you from the center of the court. Always force him to the left wing or the right wing. The reason is simple; taking a shot from the center has a higher success percentage than taking it from an angle.

So when you are playing man to man always stand at an angle so your opponent finds it harder to sneak in to the center.

Blocking with the Elbows

As you block the player you must block him with arms raised and elbows behind you, unlike when you are facing an opponent with the ball where you spread your arms wide behind you. This enables you to block the opponent with your forearm and makes it difficult for him to tackle and come forward.

General Tips

Although most coaches have their own theories and principles, nearly all coaches expect the following from a defender:

- Get your hand up to contest every shot.

- Try your best to keep your defender in front of you (not let them get around you).

- Box out all the time.

- Put in your best effort.

DEFENSIVE CONCLUSION: If you follow all of these techniques and principles, and then follow whatever instructions your coach gives you, you will be an ultimate defender!

Athleticism

No matter how good your technique and skills are, if you face a more athletic player than yourself, you are going to have some troubles. *Being able to jump high, run quickly, and have sufficient strength are extremely important when it comes to being a great basketball player.* Luckily, all of these qualities can be improved.

The main exercises that are used to improve your strength, vertical jump and speed, go hand in hand; what improves one, will also improve another.

First, we're going to explain you how to jump higher and run quicker. Strength will tie in with these topics!

So **how do I jump higher and run quicker?**

There are many different ways to jump higher and run quicker, however, we're going to share with you general principles that have helped millions of people increase their vertical jumps, run quicker, and become top athletes. Many NCAA and NBA players have followed these principles. If you follow them as well, we can promise you that your vertical jump and speed will have no choice but to increase!

The secret to jumping and running quick can be found in basic physics. Increasing your vertical jump and speed comes down to one simple concept. **Increase your overall power-to-body weight ratio**. If you can do this, your vertical jump and speed will scientifically have to increase.

What Is Power?

Power = Force x Velocity

Force is the maximum amount of **strength** that someone has and *velocity* is the maximum amount of **speed** someone has. If you increase your strength and your velocity (in ratio to your body weight) then your vertical jump and speed will improve. This is the general principle that millions of top athletes have followed. It is that simple!

What Is Strength?

The most effective way to measure your strength when it comes to the vertical jump and speed are exercises like the *full Olympic back squat, front squat, powerlifting style squat, box squat,* and *deadlift*. **Increase the amount of weight**

you can lift in any of these exercises in comparison to your bodyweight and you vertical jump and speed will increase.

NOTE: How to do these exercises will be explained under *Drills and Exercises*.

What Is Velocity?

Velocity is the speed at which the vertical jump is done and how quick your strides are when running. The vertical jump is a very quick movement. On average, most vertical jumps happen around .2 seconds. Having quick velocity allows you to display your strength. Effective ways at increasing your velocity are exercises like *depth jumps, shock jumps, broad jumps, jumping,* and *sprinting*.

NOTE: How to do these exercises will be explained under *Drills and Exercises*.

To better understand these principles here are some examples.

Example 1

Athlete A: Bodyweight 150 lbs., Maximum Squat 300 lbs., Maximum Power in the Vertical Jump 275 lbs.

Athlete B: Bodyweight 150 lbs., Maximum Squat 300 lbs., Maximum Power in the Vertical Jump 150lbs.

Both of these athletes weigh the same and can squat the same, however, in the quick movement of the vertical jump, Athlete A puts out 275lbs. of force and Athlete B only puts out 150lbs. of force. Therefore, **Athlete A will jump higher than Athlete B**. Athlete B will have to increase his Velocity to allow his strength to carry over into his vertical jump and make his vertical increase.

Example 2

Athlete A: Bodyweight 150 lbs., Maximum squat 300 lbs., Maximum Power in the vertical jump 290 lbs.

Athlete B: Bodyweight 250 lbs., Maximum squat 300lbs., Maximum Power in the vertical jump 290 lbs.

Both of these athletes can squat the same and put out the same maximum power in the vertical jump, however, Athlete A weighs 100 pounds less than Athlete B. Therefore, **Athlete A** has a better power-to-weight ratio and **will be able throw himself into the air higher**. If athlete B wanted to jump higher he could lose some weight.

Example 3

Athlete A: Bodyweight 150 lbs., Maximum squat 150 lbs., Maximum Power in the vertical jump 150 lbs.

Athlete B: Bodyweight 150 lbs., Maximum squat 400lbs., Maximum Power in the vertical jump 375 lbs.

Which one of these athletes can jump higher?

If you answered athlete B, then you are learning! **Athlete B can jump much higher than athlete A** because he has much more strength and can display most of that strength with his quick velocity in the vertical jump. If athlete A wanted to increase his vertical jump he would have to increase his maximum squat and continue to increase his velocity so that he can display his strength in his vertical jump.

Besides having leg strength, it is also important to develop strength in the upper body. Exercises like the *bench press, pull ups, chin ups, military press,* and *barbell rows* will help increase your upper body strength.

Conditioning

Being able to run up and down the court without getting tired is essential to being a great basketball player. If you get too tired when you are playing you won't be able to think properly, or execute any of the movements that you have to.

There are two important tests that you can use to determine if you are in good enough shape to handle the rigorous requirements of playing a game of full court basketball. If you can pass these tests, then you are in good enough shape to play basketball at a high level.

Not only are these tests, but they can also be used as a training method to increase your conditioning. By simply attempting to do the tests, you will improve your endurance and conditioning.

Test 1: Kansas City Basketball Conditioning Test

Step 1: Line up on the baseline.

Step 2: Sprint to opposite baseline, sprint back to starting baseline, sprint to opposite baseline again, then sprint back towards starting baseline and stop at free throw line. Finish entire sprint within 22 seconds.

Step 3: Rest 22 seconds.

Step 4: Perform a total of 20 reps.

If you can **complete this test** you are on par with some of the top NCAA and NBA players in the world. This is an extremely difficult test and you should be very proud of yourself if you can accomplish it. If you cannot finish the reps in 22 seconds or less, than do them as quick as you can and finish out the full 20 reps.

Test 2: 1 Mile Run

For this test, you simply run 1 mile as quick as you can and time yourself. Every time you do the test try to get a quicker time.

10 Minutes or above – You are out of shape and need to run more.

8-9 Minutes – You are in good enough shape to play a game of basketball, but not at a very high level or for a long time.

7-8 Minutes – You are in good basketball shape. Not elite, but good enough to play hard for a while.

6-7 Minutes – You are in great basketball shape. You can play hard and for a long time.

5-6 Minutes – You are in top, NBA, basketball shape. You are most likely in better shape than anyone you play against. Rip Hamilton, NBA player known for being in great shape, can complete the run in roughly 5 minutes.

Under 5 Minutes – You should be a runner! You are in phenomenal shape.

Recovery and Injury prevention

Static and dynamic stretches are extremely important when it comes to preventing injuries and recovering.

What is Dynamic Stretching?

Dynamic stretching uses speed of a movement and momentum to stretch a muscle. For example, swinging your leg side to side is a dynamic stretch. Dynamic stretches will be done before a workout to help you warm up.

What is Static Stretching?

Static stretching is keeping the body at rest and staying in one position while stretching a muscle. For example, leaning over and touching your toes, and then holding that position for a certain amount of time without moving. This type of stretching will be done at some point after your workout and on off days.

NOTE: Specific stretches will be explained under *Drills and Exercises*.

DRILLS AND EXERCISES

The drills and exercises are based off everything you just learned. They will be separated into dribbling, passing, shooting, defense, athleticism, and recovery and injury prevention.

1. *RECOVERY AND INJURY PREVENTION* - **DYNAMIC WARMUP.**

   These will be done before all basketball drills or weightlifting exercises.

   NOTE: It will be listed in the actual program when to do them.

   – **Stationary squats** 10 reps

- **Walking lunges** 5 reps per each leg

- **Side leg swings** 10 reps per each leg

- **Front leg swings** 10 reps per each leg

- **Toe touches** 10 reps

- **Power Skipping to half court and back**

- **High knees to half court and back**

- **Butt kicks to half court and back**

- **Jog full court and back** 2 reps

- **Defensive slide half court and back**

  In the position on your left you must run from one side of the court to another and back as fast as possible. You can go from back line to free throw line or back line to centre line. You must stay low throughout and tap the ground on each side.

- **60% sprint full court**

  Starting at the baseline, sprint 60% of the way down the court. Then slow down and stop before reaching the opposite baseline.

- **70% sprint full court**

- **80% sprint full court**

- **5 stationary jump and lands (75-80% effort)**

By the time you are done this warm up, you should have broken and sweat and feel completely loose and ready to go.

2. *RECOVERY AND INJURY PREVENTION* - **STATIC STRETCHING.**

This will be done after your workouts and on off days. It will help maintain/increase your flexibility and assist you in recovering fully for next workouts. Get a timer and hold the stretches for the given amount of time. Don't cheat!

— **Hip flexor stretch** 1 minute per each side

- **Sitting hamstring stretch** 1 minute

- **Sitting Quad stretch** 2 minutes

- **Lying Gluteus stretch** 1 minute per leg

- **Calf stretch** 1 minute per leg

- **Side splits attempt** 30 seconds

- **Front splits attempt** 30 seconds per leg

3. *DRIBBLING* - BALL HANDLING CIRCUIT.

This will drastically improve your dribbling skills. The entire circuit should be finished in 5-10 min. Make sure to do every exercise as quick as possible, with your head up, and be under control. If you lose control of the ball sometimes that is good! It means you are pushing yourself.

Take a look at *"Ball Handling and Dribbling"* chapter for description of these dribbles.

I want you to go through the whole chapter before you start your practice.

- **Finger taps and slaps** 30 seconds
  Tap and slap the basketball with your fingers for warm-up

- **Continuous circles around head, waist, legs**
  Do the circles with the ball around your head, waist and legs, change direction after 5 reps

- **Control dribble waist** 20 reps

- **Control dribble above head** 20 reps

- **Power dribble** 20 reps
  Dribble between legs while walking or brisk walking. Increase your speed, change angles, practice with zigzag walking patterns or figure 8s. Put as much variation in your drill to increase efficacy.

- **Stationary crossovers alternating between long and close** 25 reps
  Dribble with one hand and then switch to the other. Dribble the ball higher then lower.

- **Stationary crossover between legs** 25 reps
  Do a crossover between your legs while standing. Change the legs.

- **Stationary dribbles behind the back** 25 reps

- **One hand pendulum dribbles forward** 20 reps per each hand

- **One hand pendulum dribbles backwards** 20 reps per each hand

- **Alternating pendulum dribbles forward/backwards/ switching hands** 10 reps

- **Rapid figure 8 dribbles forward** 5 reps

- **Rapid figure 8 dribbles backwards** 5 reps

4. *DRIBBLING* - BASIC 3 DRIBBLING TRANSITION.

This will work on the basic 3 dribbles and help you be able to transition between them.

Speed dribble to half court, Control dribble to 3 point line, Power dribble to baseline. Walk back to other side of court. 5 reps

5. *DRIBBLING* - DRIVE AND JAB FAKE DRIVES.

This will work on your drive and jab fake drives.

You are going to drive both left and right from 5 total spots around the 3 point line.

- Spin the ball to yourself, catch it and put it into your triple threat position, then **drive right** and do a layup. Get your rebound, go back to the same spot and **drive left** and do a layup. Once you go both left and right from a single spot, move onto the next spot. You are finished when you have done a *total of 10 reps.*

- Catch your breath then do repeat the exact same thing, however, this time, do **jab fake drives** instead.

6. *DRIBBLING –* **CROSSOVER CIRCUIT.**

This will work on your crossovers. Make sure to try to move the ball as quick as you can, and keep your head up. You will take a few dribbles, do a crossover, then take a few more dribbles and do another crossover, and keep going the entire length of the court. Do 2 reps of each exercise.

Take a look at *"Ball Handling and Dribbling"* chapter for description of these dribbles.

I want you to go through the whole chapter again before you start your practice.

- **Full court & back regular crossovers**

- **Full court & back between legs crossovers**

- **Full court & back behind the back crossovers**

- **Full court & back spin crossovers**

- **Full court & back in and out crossovers**

- **Full court & back double crossovers (any combination you want)**

- **Full court & back triple crossovers (any combination you want)**

7. *SHOOTING* - **POST SKILLS CIRCUIT.**

This will help you finish around the rim. The objective is to make as many lay-ups as possible. Do at least 25 reps for each of these drills.

— **Mikan drill**

- Stand on one side of the basket inside of the block facing the baseline. Jump and power the ball up for a lay-up. Make sure to use the backboard on each shot

- After landing, jump back up and rebound the ball out of the net. Try to rebound the ball at its highest point. When you grab the ball, be sure to keep it above your head

- Your jump should transition you to the other side of the basket. If you jumped from the right side, it should take you over to the left side

- Jump and power the ball up for a lay-up on the opposite side in a continuous motion

- Continue the process from side to side, working on both your right and left hand lay-ups

- Jump off one leg by exploding towards the basket on each shot.

— **Reverse Mikan drill**
Perform Mikan drill with your back to the baseline instead of facing the baseline and execute a reverse lay-up

— **Two ball Mikan drill**
Perform Mikan drill holding two balls in your hands.

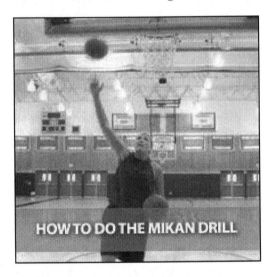

— **Two ball reverse Mikan drill**

Perform two ball Mikan drill with your back to the baseline instead of facing the baseline and execute a reverse lay-up

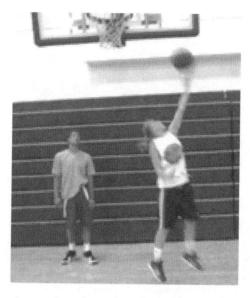

8. *SHOOTING*- **STATIONARY FORM SHOOTING.**
Focus on the basketball shooting technique that was taught earlier.

- **Straight on shots**
  Go right up to the net and shoot 10 shots straight on

- **Shot from the left**
  Step left from the rim and take 10 shots

- **Shot from the right**
  Step right from the rim and take 10 shots

9. *SHOOTING* – **HALF COURT TO FREE THROW JUMP SHOTS.**

Pull up jump shot from free throw line
Dribble from half court to the free throw line and shoot a pull up jump shot. Do 20 reps.

10. *SHOOTING -* 1-2-3 FIVE BLOCK CIRCUIT.

This drill will be shot in 5 different blocks. Once you are done one block, you go to the next one without taking any breaks.

- Pick any block and start at point 1. Shoot a **regular set shot**. You keep shooting until you make three in a row.

- You then go to point 2 and shoot **pull up jump shots**. You don't stop until you make three in a row.

- You then go to point 3 and shoot **regular 3 point shots**. You don't stop until you make 3 in a row.

- Once you completed a block, you move to the next block. Finish *all 5 blocks*.

11. *SHOOTING -* SHOOT 25 FREE THROWS.

Don't forget about the lessons learnt from Michael Jordan on the free throw shooting.

12. *DEFENSE -* DEFENSIVE CIRCUIT.

Take a look at the *"Defense"* chapter for description of defensive slides.

I want you to go through the whole chapter before you start your practice. Do 2 reps of each of these drills.

- **Defensive slide from baseline to baseline**
  In the position on your left you must run from one side of the court to another and back as fast as possible. You must stay low throughout and tap the ground on each side

- **Defensive slide zig-zag the entire length of the court**
  Pivot and change directions every time you do 5 slides

13. *PASSING –* PASSING CIRCUIT.

Find a wall and make a target on it.

- **Chess passes against the wall**
  Do 25 chest passes against the wall, progressively moving further out. Go as far as you can until you can't hit the target anymore

- **Bounce passes against the wall**
  Do 25 bounce passes against the wall and progressively move further out until you can't hit the target anymore

- **Overhead passes against the wall**
  Do 25 overhead passes against the wall and progressively move further out until you can't hit the target anymore

14. *CONDITIONING –* 1 MILE RUN.

Make sure you time yourself.

Check you results against the *Test 2* described in *"Conditioning"* chapter.

15. *CONDITIONING –* KANSAS CITY BASKETBALL CONDITIONING TEST.

Step 1: Line up on the baseline.

Step 2: Sprint to opposite baseline, sprint back to starting baseline, sprint to opposite baseline again, then sprint back towards starting baseline and stop at free throw line. Finish entire sprint within 22 seconds.

Step 3:   Rest 22 seconds.

Step 4:   Perform a total of 20 reps.

Read more on "*Conditioning*" section.

16. *ATHLETECISM* – FULL OLYMPIC BACK SQUAT.

You want to make sure you add weight to this every week. Do 3 sets of 6 reps.

17. *ATHLETECISM* - FRONT SQUAT.

You want to make sure you add weight to this every week. Do 4 sets of 4 reps.

18. *ATHLETECISM* – BENCH PRESS.

You want to make sure you add weight to this every week. Do 3 sets of 5 reps.

19. *ATHLETECISM* – PULL UP/CHIN UP CIRCUIT.

Maximum amount of pull-ups you can do. Take a 2 min. break and then do the maximum amount of chin-ups you can do.

20. *ATHLETECISM* – BARBELL ROW.

You want to make sure you add weight to this every week. Do 3 sets of 5 reps.

21. *ATHLETECISM* - **MILITARY PRESS**.

For this exercise you lift the bar over your head. You want to make sure you add weight to this every week. Do 3 sets of 5 reps.

22. *ATHLETECISM* – **MAX EFFORT JUMP**.

Take 3 steps and jump as high as you can. Do 5 reps.

23. *ATHLETECISM* – **MAX EFFORT STATIONARY JUMPS**.

Stand still and jump as high as you can. Do 5 reps.

THE 21-DAY PROGRAM

This program will use drills and exercises that will specifically increase you dribbling, passing, shooting, conditioning, and athleticism. *Each number in the program is coordinated with the same number under the Drills and Exercises section*. Therefore, in order to understand what to do for each exercise or drill, find and match the numbers for each day with the same number under the Drills and Exercises category.

You may want to make a copy of "The 21-Day Program" and cross off each exercise after you complete it.

If at any point you feel completely beat up, exhausted, and don't feel like working out, take the day off. You are overworked and need to recover!

If you try your best, but can't add any weight to your exercises every week because it is too heavy, eat more food! Getting enough protein, carbohydrates, and healthy fats are essential to recovering. This is an intense session so you would want to take good care of your nutrition. You know you are eating enough if you feel energized and are able to gain strength every week. Also keep a bottle of electrolytes nearby, such as Gatorade or a bottle of Tang, when you practice.

No amount of drills can be compared with a competitive game to test and develop team coordination and passing skills. *You must be playing at least two complete games every week*.

Have fun and good luck improving your basketball game!

DAY 1:

a) Drill #1 <u>Dynamic Warm Up</u>

b) Drill #22 <u>Max Effort Jump</u>

c) Drill #16 <u>Full Olympic Back Squat</u>

d) Drill #3 <u>Ball Handling Circuit</u>

e) Drill #4 <u>Basic 3 Dribbling Transition</u>

f) Drill #5 <u>Drive And Jab Fake Drives</u>

g) Drill #6 <u>Crossover Circuit</u>

h) Drill #7 <u>Post Skills Circuit</u>

i) Drill #8 <u>Stationary Form Shooting</u>

j) Drill #9 <u>Half Court To Free Throw Jump Shots</u>

k) Drill #10 <u>1-2-3 Five Block Circuit</u>

l) Drill #11 <u>Shoot 25 Free Throws</u>

m) Drill #12 <u>Defensive Circuit</u>

n) Drill #13 <u>Passing Circuit</u>

o) Drill #2 <u>Static Stretching</u>

DAY 2:

a) Drill #1 <u>Dynamic Warm Up</u>

b) Drill #18 <u>Bench Press</u>

c) Drill #19 <u>Pull Up/Chin Up Circuit</u>

d) Drill #20 <u>Barbell Row</u>

e) Drill #21 Military Press

f) Drill #3 Ball Handling Circuit

g) Drill #4 Basic 3 Dribbling Transition

h) Drill #5 Drive And Jab Fake Drives

i) Drill #6 Crossover Circuit

j) Drill #7 Post Skills Circuit

k) Drill #8 Stationary Form Shooting

l) Drill #9 Half Court To Free Throw Jump Shots

m) Drill #10 1-2-3 Five Block Circuit

n) Drill #11 Shoot 25 Free Throws

o) Drill #12 Defensive Circuit

p) Drill #13 Passing Circuit

q) Drill #2 Static Stretching

DAY 3:

a) Drill #1 Dynamic Warm Up

b) Drill #15 Kansas City Basketball Conditioning Test

c) Drill #3 Ball Handling Circuit

d) Drill #4 Basic 3 Dribbling Transition

e) Drill #5 Drive And Jab Fake Drives

f) Drill #6 Crossover Circuit

g) Drill #7 Post Skills Circuit

h) Drill #8 <u>Stationary Form Shooting</u>

i) Drill #9 <u>Half Court To Free Throw Jump Shots</u>

j) Drill #10 <u>1-2-3 Five Block Circuit</u>

k) Drill #11 <u>Shoot 25 Free Throws</u>

l) Drill #12 <u>Defensive Circuit</u>

m) Drill #13 <u>Passing Circuit</u>

n) Drill #2 <u>Static Stretching</u>

DAY 4:

a) Drill #1 <u>Dynamic Warm Up</u>

b) Drill #14 <u>1 Mile Run</u>

c) Drill #2 <u>Static Stretching</u>

DAY 5:

a) Drill #1 <u>Dynamic Warm Up</u>

b) Drill #23 <u>Max Effort Stationary Jumps</u>

c) Drill #3 <u>Ball Handling Circuit</u>

d) Drill #4 <u>Basic 3 Dribbling Transition</u>

e) Drill #5 <u>Drive And Jab Fake Drives</u>

f) Drill #6 <u>Crossover Circuit</u>

g) Drill #7 <u>Post Skills Circuit</u>

h) Drill #8 <u>Stationary Form Shooting</u>

i) Drill #9 <u>Half Court To Free Throw Jump Shots</u>

j)   Drill #10 <u>1-2-3 Five Block Circuit</u>

k)   Drill #11 <u>Shoot 25 Free Throws</u>

l)   Drill #12 <u>Defensive Circuit</u>

m)   Drill #13 <u>Passing Circuit</u>

n)   Drill #2 <u>Static Stretching</u>

DAY 6:

a)   Drill #2 <u>Static Stretching</u>

DAY 7:

Off day.

DAY 8:

a)   Drill #1 <u>Dynamic Warm Up</u>

b)   Drill #22 <u>Max Effort Jump</u>

c)   Drill #16 <u>Full Olympic Back Squat</u>

d)   Drill #3 <u>Ball Handling Circuit</u>

e)   Drill #4 <u>Basic 3 Dribbling Transition</u>

f)   Drill #5 <u>Drive And Jab Fake Drives</u>

g)   Drill #6 <u>Crossover Circuit</u>

h)   Drill #7 <u>Post Skills Circuit</u>

i)   Drill #8 <u>Stationary Form Shooting</u>

j)   Drill #9 <u>Half Court To Free Throw Jump Shots</u>

k) Drill #10 <u>1-2-3 Five Block Circuit</u>

l) Drill #11 <u>Shoot 25 Free Throws</u>

m) Drill #12 <u>Defensive Circuit</u>

n) Drill #13 <u>Passing Circuit</u>

o) Drill #2 <u>Static Stretching</u>

DAY 9:

a) Drill #1 <u>Dynamic Warm Up</u>

b) Drill #18 <u>Bench Press</u>

c) Drill #19 <u>Pull Up/Chin Up Circuit</u>

d) Drill #20 <u>Barbell Row</u>

e) Drill #21 <u>Military Press</u>

f) Drill #3 <u>Ball Handling Circuit</u>

g) Drill #4 <u>Basic 3 Dribbling Transition</u>

h) Drill #5 <u>Drive And Jab Fake Drives</u>

i) Drill #6 <u>Crossover Circuit</u>

j) Drill #7 <u>Post Skills Circuit</u>

k) Drill #8 <u>Stationary Form Shooting</u>

l) Drill #9 <u>Half Court To Free Throw Jump Shots</u>

m) Drill #10 <u>1-2-3 Five Block Circuit</u>

n) Drill #11 <u>Shoot 25 Free Throws</u>

o) Drill #12 <u>Defensive Circuit</u>

p)   Drill #13 Passing Circuit

q)   Drill #2 Static Stretching

DAY 10:

a)   Drill #1 Dynamic Warm Up

b)   Drill #15 Kansas City Basketball Conditioning Test

c)   Drill #3 Ball Handling Circuit

d)   Drill #4 Basic 3 Dribbling Transition

e)   Drill #5 Drive And Jab Fake Drives

f)   Drill #6 Crossover Circuit

g)   Drill #7 Post Skills Circuit

h)   Drill #8 Stationary Form Shooting

i)   Drill #9 Half Court To Free Throw Jump Shots

j)   Drill #10 1-2-3 Five Block Circuit

k)   Drill #11 Shoot 25 Free Throws

l)   Drill #12 Defensive Circuit

m) Drill #13 Passing Circuit

n)   Drill #2 Static Stretching

DAY 11:

a)   Drill #1 Dynamic Warm Up

b)   Drill #14 1 Mile Run

c)   Drill #2 Static Stretching

DAY 12:

a) Drill #1 Dynamic Warm Up

b) Drill #23 Max Effort Stationary Jumps

c) Drill #3 Ball Handling Circuit

d) Drill #4 Basic 3 Dribbling Transition

e) Drill #5 Drive And Jab Fake Drives

f) Drill #6 Crossover Circuit

g) Drill #7 Post Skills Circuit

h) Drill #8 Stationary Form Shooting

i) Drill #9 Half Court To Free Throw Jump Shots

j) Drill #10 1-2-3 Five Block Circuit

k) Drill #11 Shoot 25 Free Throws

l) Drill #12 Defensive Circuit

m) Drill #13 Passing Circuit

n) Drill #2 Static Stretching

DAY 13:

a) Drill #2 Static Stretching

DAY 14:

Off day.

DAY 15:

a) Drill #1 <u>Dynamic Warm Up</u>

b) Drill #22 <u>Max Effort Jump</u>

c) Drill #16 <u>Full Olympic Back Squat</u>

d) Drill #3 <u>Ball Handling Circuit</u>

e) Drill #4 <u>Basic 3 Dribbling Transition</u>

f) Drill #5 <u>Drive And Jab Fake Drives</u>

g) Drill #6 <u>Crossover Circuit</u>

h) Drill #7 <u>Post Skills Circuit</u>

i) Drill #8 <u>Stationary Form Shooting</u>

j) Drill #9 <u>Half Court To Free Throw Jump Shots</u>

k) Drill #10 <u>1-2-3 Five Block Circuit</u>

l) Drill #11 <u>Shoot 25 Free Throws</u>

m) Drill #12 <u>Defensive Circuit</u>

n) Drill #13 <u>Passing Circuit</u>

o) Drill #2 <u>Static Stretching</u>

DAY 16:

a) Drill #1 <u>Dynamic Warm Up</u>

b) Drill #18 <u>Bench Press</u>

c) Drill #19 <u>Pull Up/Chin Up Circuit</u>

d) Drill #20 <u>Barbell Row</u>

e) Drill #21 Military Press

f) Drill #3 Ball Handling Circuit

g) Drill #4 Basic 3 Dribbling Transition

h) Drill #5 Drive And Jab Fake Drives

i) Drill #6 Crossover Circuit

j) Drill #7 Post Skills Circuit

k) Drill #8 Stationary Form Shooting

l) Drill #9 Half Court To Free Throw Jump Shots

m) Drill #10 1-2-3 Five Block Circuit

n) Drill #11 Shoot 25 Free Throws

o) Drill #12 Defensive Circuit

p) Drill #13 Passing Circuit

q) Drill #2 Static Stretching

DAY 17:

a) Drill #1 Dynamic Warm Up

b) Drill #15 Kansas City Basketball Conditioning Test

c) Drill #3 Ball Handling Circuit

d) Drill #4 Basic 3 Dribbling Transition

e) Drill #5 Drive And Jab Fake Drives

f) Drill #6 Crossover Circuit

g) Drill #7 Post Skills Circuit

h) Drill #8 <u>Stationary Form Shooting</u>

i) Drill #9 <u>Half Court To Free Throw Jump Shots</u>

j) Drill #10 <u>1-2-3 Five Block Circuit</u>

k) Drill #11 <u>Shoot 25 Free Throws</u>

l) Drill #12 <u>Defensive Circuit</u>

m) Drill #13 <u>Passing Circuit</u>

n) Drill #2 <u>Static Stretching</u>

DAY 18:

a) Drill #1 <u>Dynamic Warm Up</u>

b) Drill #14 <u>1 Mile Run</u>

c) Drill #2 <u>Static Stretching</u>

DAY 19:

a) Drill #1 <u>Dynamic Warm Up</u>

b) Drill #23 <u>Max Effort Stationary Jumps</u>

c) Drill #3 <u>Ball Handling Circuit</u>

d) Drill #4 <u>Basic 3 Dribbling Transition</u>

e) Drill #5 <u>Drive And Jab Fake Drives</u>

f) Drill #6 <u>Crossover Circuit</u>

g) Drill #7 <u>Post Skills Circuit</u>

h) Drill #8 <u>Stationary Form Shooting</u>

i) Drill #9 <u>Half Court To Free Throw Jump Shots</u>

j)   Drill #10 <u>1-2-3 Five Block Circuit</u>

k)   Drill #11 <u>Shoot 25 Free Throws</u>

l)   Drill #12 <u>Defensive Circuit</u>

m)   Drill #13 <u>Passing Circuit</u>

n)   Drill #2 <u>Static Stretching</u>

DAY 20:

a)   Drill #2 <u>Static Stretching</u>

DAY 21:

Off day.

CONCLUSION

Congratulations! You have finished the program by working hard in the past 21 days.

You have learned how to improve your shooting, dribbling, passing, defense, athleticism, conditioning, and how to prevent injuries and recover. Not only did you learn how to do this, but you have actually went out and done it! I am sure that by this stage your practice sessions have moved beyond one-on-one practices to actual friendly games.

If you want to continue to see improvements you could do the program a second time through. Simply start at Day 1 again!

Let's recap some major lessons learned throughout this book and what better way to do that than through the teachings of basketball legends.

Important Lessons from Basketball Legends

- John Wooden won 10 NCAA championships coaching at UCLA. He taught players such as Kareem Abdul-Jabbar and Bill Walton. 24 of his players made it to All American. John always stressed that *every player should be in peak condition*. Teach them the value of the game and the fundamentals. Hit the open man on offense and drill the values of team play. Defense is hard work and takes time to build but offense should not be solely responsible for winning.

- Kareem Abdul-Jabbar said about Coach Wooden: "The biggest lesson I learned from him was *preparation*." Kareem went on to become the leading all time scorer in NBA with 38387 points! He followed the advice through and through by training with coaches as diverse as Bruce Lee.

- Magic Johnson is a retired American Professional Basketball player who played for the Lakers. He was rated as the greatest NBA point guard of all time by ESPN 2007, was a member of the Dream Team and is honored as one of the 50 Greatest NBA Players in History. The legend had to undergo major struggle in his life due to HIV. However, he dedicated his life to increasing AIDS awareness and philanthropy. His message is simple, *tolerance for each other*.

- And lastly, we have Michael Jordan, the greatest North American athlete of the 20th Century by ESPN and second only to Babe Ruth on Associated Press's list of athletes of the century. His biggest message to us all is that *"in life you get what you expect and accept. If you answer these questions you will change your life."*

Prep Talk

Whatever the nature or type of sport, be it baseball, football, basketball etc., nothing motivates a team better then a strong coach; one who has principles, is able to draw the performance out of you and knows the right thing to say at the right time.

A seasoned basketball team in the lockers about to step out in the court might be feeling confident. However, an excellent prep talk can mean the difference between a good performance and an extraordinary game. Although there are many types of prep talks your coach can give you, since this is your own program we want you to take the reins here and visualize...

- Tell yourself how hard you have been practicing for the past 21 days.

- Tell yourself the time you had taken out and compromises made. Think about what this game means to you.

- Also think about the opponent, how it has lost or won against you? What are their weaknesses?

- Now visualize, close your eyes and take nice deep breaths while imagining the game.

- Imagine yourself rushing out of the lockers and as you hit the court the crowd erupts in a chorus.

- You can sense the smell of the court and the temperature on your skin, yes, you are at right place, and you are very comfortable in the court because you spend most of your time here, at practice and other games. This is your territory and the opponent does not have a chance.

- Now imagine, the referee's whistle, the ball is tossed in the air and your offense jumps and get possession of the ball. The opponent does not stand a chance.

- Repeatedly you shoot, dunk and dodge the ball in the basket.

- You smile at the opponents, you respect them but you are here to win and repeatedly you make the basket and block their shots if any.

- You steamroll over them!

Now that you are trained, focused and prepared it's time to rock and roll! Play to win!

ABOUT THE AUTHOR

James Wilson is a certified personal trainer and professional basketball coach. He has been developing young basketball players to excel in their game for over 30 years. He has worked with coaches and basketball players in more than 20 countries worldwide, which has enabled him to develop a unique playing style and coaching method.

His coaching philosophy revolves on three fundamental concepts: "best possible player conditioning", "quickness" and "conviction". These key points should be followed in every aspect of the game but when they are followed in every aspect of life, a basketball player can become truly great.

There are thousands of drills that can be practiced to improve your basketball game. Even NBA players can not pinpoint the exact programs that should be selected or discarded. However, with experience, seasoned coaches can give a guideline of drills most useful at the start of a new season. Thus, this book can be looked as a summation of the most important lessons the author has meticulously taught his students over 30 years of his life.

Made in the USA
Lexington, KY
23 April 2018